BEST PRACTICES FOR LOW-LIGHT
PHOTOGRAPHY 71

VIDEOGRAPHY TIPS 76

EDITING AND POST-PROCESSING 88

IMPORTING AND ORGANIZING FOOTAGE ... 88

CHAPTER FOUR 92

BASIC EDITING TOOLS AND TECHNIQUES 92

ADDING EFFECTS AND MUSIC 95

USING INSTA360 STUDIO ON DESKTOP 99

STITCHING AND EXPORTING 360 VIDEOS .. 104

ENHANCING PHOTOS WITH EXTERNAL
SOFTWARE 108

SHARING YOUR CREATIONS 112

TIPS FOR ENGAGING CONTENT 118

VIRTUAL REALITY 120

VIEWING YOUR 360 CONTENT IN VR 121

SHARING VR EXPERIENCES WITH FRIENDS 123

CHAPTER FIVE 127

ACCESSORIES AND ENHANCEMENTS 127

RECOMMENDED TRIPODS AND MOUNTS . 128

ENHANCING YOUR EXPERIENCE YOUR 360
EXPERIENCE 133

USING EXTERNAL MICROPHONES.............133

TROUBLESHOOTING AND MAINTENANCE .140

MAINTAINING YOUR CAMERA...................147

ENSURING LONGEVITY OF YOUR INSTA360 X4
....151

EXPERT GUIDE ON USING THE INSTA360 X4
FOR RIDES 153

CHAPTER SIX 156

RECORDING AND SHARING YOUR RIDE 156

SHOOTING TIPS FOR EVERY SCENARIO 161

TRAVEL AND CREATIVE VIDEOGRAPHY......161

BIKING 166

WINTER SPORTS..168

DRIVING 169

SNORKELING WITH THE INSTA360 X4........170

CHAPTER SEVEN..183

HOW TO LIVE STREAM AND APPLY
STABILIZATION WITH YOUR INSTA360 X4..183

LIVE STREAMING WITH INSTA360 X4.........184

APPLYING STABILIZATION WITH INSTA360 X4
....188

HOW TO USE THE INVISIBLE SELFIE STICK
FEATURE ON YOUR INSTA360 X4 194

WHEN TO USE THE INVISIBLE SELFIE STICK 200

COMPETITION AND LAST THOUGHTS 204

THE END 208

CHAPTER ONE

INTRODUCTION

360-degree photography has had a most amazing journey. A complete spherical view was first a difficult and expensive task that frequently required several cameras and a lot of post-processing. Still, the introduction of digital photography and developments in camera technology has fundamentally changed this environment.

First attempts at 360-degree photography required laborious setups with several cameras connected to record various views, which were then stitched together with specialist software. Time-consuming as it was, this procedure was also costly and only available to experts with substantial resources.

The invention of small, easily portable 360 cameras was the turning point. Leading this market were Ricoh, Samsung, and GoPro, with their Theta, Gear 360, and Fusion versions, in that order. These cameras had dual-lens systems that could record fully spherical photos and films with little post-processing needed.

A flood of cutting-edge 360 cameras with improved user interfaces, better stabilization, and sharper resolution have entered the market lately. Leading innovator Insta360 is one example, having continuously pushed the envelope of what is feasible in 360-degree photography. Their offerings, which comprise the Insta360 ONE R and X, have raised the bar for usability and performance.

OVERVIEW OF THE INSTA360 X4

The Insta360 X4 is the most advanced 360-degree camera available, intended for both pros and enthusiasts. This camera is a great option for everyone wishing to start exploring immersive photography and filmmaking because it combines state-of-the-art features with easy-to-use operation.

Important Information about the Insta360 X4:

System of Two Lenses: Together, the X4's two high-resolution lenses record smooth 360-degree video.

5.7K Pixels Driven by a brand-new 5nm AI chip, experience moments like they were your first time and immerse yourself in amazing clarity. Every action frame and color streak with before unheard-of detail.

VIDEO 5.7K60FPS 360°

HIGHER FRAME RATES,

Enjoy 60 frames per second at a smoother, clearer image for every frame! Perfect for heavily moving scenarios or action sports. Put it at 4K100fps for cinematic slow motion!

72MP 360° PHOTO - LOTS OF PIXELS

Take captivating 360-degree pictures that will have you staring.

72-megapixel images with previously unheard-of levels of sharpness and detail

FlowState Stabilization: Even in hectic and fast-paced settings, Insta360's in-house stabilization technology guarantees smooth and steady video.

Better color and contrast made possible by High Dynamic Range (HDR) mode enhance the vibrancy and real-life quality of your images and movies.

AI Editing Tools: With a few touches, the Insta360 app's collection of AI-powered editing tools enables you to quickly produce footage of the highest caliber. Hit record and discover the ideal shot with the Insta360 app's AI-powered reframing features.

Live Streaming: The X4 enables you to post your travels in real-time on social media sites with your audience.

Waterproof Design: The X4 is ideal for underwater photography and filmmaking since it is weatherproof up to ten meters.

UNBOXING AND SETUP

What's in the Box?

Receiving your Insta360 X4 is like opening a door to a whole new creative world. Everything you need to begin shooting and filming 360-degree photos and videos is included in the package.

Inside the Box:

Attain 360 X4 Camera The main attraction, this stylish, little gadget is made to record amazing 360-degree photos and videos.

- Protective Case: A robust case to safeguard your camera both in transit and storage.
- Powering your camera is a rechargeable lithium-ion battery.
- Data transfer and battery charge are accomplished with a USB-C cable.
- Optional MicroSD Card: A high-speed microSD card is a must for storing your pictures and movies and may be included in some packages.

- Lens Cloth: Use this gentle cloth to keep the smudges and dirt off of your camera lenses.
- Concise instructions to help you quickly set up your camera and begin going.

INITIAL SETUP AND CHARGING

Before you begin capturing immersive 360-degree content, make sure your camera is properly set up and completely charged.

To insert the battery, locate the compartment on the camera's side or bottom.

Open the compartment and insert the battery, making sure it is securely in place.

Charge the battery.

Plug the USB-C charging cable into the camera's charging port.

Connect the other end to a power source, such as a wall adapter or a USB connection on your computer.

Allow the battery to charge completely before using the camera for the first time. The LED indicator will display the charging state, usually turning green when completely charged.

Insert a MicroSD card:

Locate the microSD card slot, which is normally near the battery compartment.

Insert the microSD card with the gold contacts facing the slot, making sure it clicks in place.

Power To activate the camera, press and hold the power button until it turns on.

Follow the on-screen prompts to finish the basic setup, which includes language selection and date/time settings.

Installing the Insta360 Application

To fully utilize your Insta360 X4, install the Insta360 app on your smartphone. The software gives users access to advanced camera settings, editing tools, and sharing choices.

Download the application:

Launch the App Store (iOS) or Google Play (Android) on your smartphone.

Search for "Insta360" and download the official app.

Pairing your camera:

Launch the Insta360 app on your smartphone.

Follow the on-screen instructions to set up an account or log in if you already have one.

Turn on the Insta360 X4 and confirm that Bluetooth and Wi-Fi are enabled.

To pair your smartphone with the camera, use the app's "Connect Camera" feature and follow the instructions. This technique usually entails scanning a QR code displayed on the camera's screen or picking the camera from a list of available options.

After connecting, the app will check for available firmware upgrades for your camera.

If an update is available, follow the instructions to download and install it. Keeping your firmware up to date gives you access to the most recent features and upgrades.

Exploring the Application:

Familiarize yourself with the app's interface and functionality. You'll be able to manage the camera remotely, modify settings, preview and transmit footage, and use editing tools.

Experiment with various shooting modes and settings to become acquainted with the app and camera.

After following these steps, you'll be ready to begin capturing breathtaking 360-degree content with your Insta360 X4. The combination of straightforward hardware and strong software offers a smooth and delightful user experience from the moment you open your camera.

CHAPTER TWO

GETTING STARTED WITH THE INSTA360 X4

CAMERA OVERVIEW AND FEATURES

The Insta360 X4 is packed with cutting-edge technology designed to make 360-degree photography and filmmaking easy and enjoyable. Here's a complete overview of its main features:

Key features:

Dual-Lens System: The X4 has two high-resolution lenses positioned back-to-back to capture everything around you in a continuous 360-degree perspective.

5.7K Resolution: Capable of recording videos in 5.7K resolution, resulting in extremely detailed and clear footage.

FlowState Stabilization: Advanced stabilization technology ensures that video is smooth and stable, even in dynamic and fast-paced circumstances.

HDR Mode: High Dynamic Range mode enhances color and contrast, making photographs more bright and lifelike.

Waterproof Design: The X4 is waterproof to 10 meters, enabling underwater photography and filmmaking without the need for a separate case.

AI Editing Tools: The Insta360 app has AI-powered editing features that make it simple to generate professional-grade content.

Live Streaming: The X4 enables live streaming, so you can share your travels in real-time.

Long Battery Life: The camera has a robust battery that provides enough recording time to capture all of your memories.

NAVIGATING THE TOUCHSCREEN INTERFACE

The Insta360 X4 features a user-friendly touchscreen interface that allows you to access and alter settings while on the go. Here's how to navigate it.

Home screen:

The home screen displays the current shooting mode, battery

life, storage space, and other important details.

Swipe left or right to select between shooting modes like photo, video, HDR, and timelapse.

To access the Settings menu, hit the gear symbol on the home screen.

You can change a variety of camera settings here, such as resolution, frame rate, ISO, and white balance.

Use the touchscreen to scroll through options and make decisions.

To enter playback mode, swipe up from the bottom of the screen.

View your images and videos straight on the camera's display.

Swipe left or right to navigate your media collection, then tap to view individual files.

Icons on the home screen offer rapid access to key features including Wi-Fi, battery status, and shooting modes.

Tap these icons to change settings or open particular menus to get additional choices.

Using the Control Buttons

In addition to the touchscreen interface, the Insta360 X4 incorporates physical control buttons that offer easy access to the following functions:

- The power button is located on the camera's side or top.
- To turn on/off the camera, press and hold.
- A fast press can also put the camera in sleep mode or wake it up.

- The shutter button is often located on the front or top of the camera.
- Press to begin or end the video recording.
- In photo mode, push to take a picture.
- Some models may include a dedicated mode button to quickly switch between shooting modes.
- Press to choose between modes such as photo, video, HDR, and timelapse.

- The Menu/Settings button opens the settings menu, allowing you to make adjustments without using the touchscreen.
- Useful for making rapid changes or wearing gloves.

Additional Tips:

Combination Presses: Some functions may necessitate pressing two buttons simultaneously. For example, resetting the camera or activating a specific mode.

Pay attention to the camera's LED indicators and sounds, which provide you feedback on your actions, such as starting/stopping recording or switching settings.

Understanding these fundamentals will help you grasp the Insta360 X4, allowing you to easily capture spectacular 360-degree content.

FIRST STEPS TO USING YOUR CAMERA

Powering on/off

To power on, locate the power button on the side or top of the Insta360 X4.

Press and Hold: Hold the power button for a few seconds until the camera turns on. The Insta360 logo will appear on the touchscreen display.

Initial Setup: The first time you turn on the camera, you may be requested to enter the language, date, and time. To finish these changes, simply follow the on-screen directions.

To switch off the camera, press and hold the power button until the screen turns dark and it shuts down.

Sleep Mode: If you fast hit the power button, the camera may go into sleep mode to save battery life. To turn it on again, press the power button.

CONNECTING TO YOUR SMARTPHONE

Connecting your Insta360 X4 to your smartphone allows you to access advanced capabilities, transfer footage, and use the Insta360 app for editing and sharing.

Step-by-Step Guidelines:

- Download the Insta360 app.
- Launch the App Store (iOS) or Google Play (Android) on your smartphone.
- Search for "Insta360" and download the official app.

- Enable Wi-Fi and Bluetooth.
- Make sure your smartphone has both Wi-Fi and Bluetooth enabled.

Power On Camera:

- Turn on your Insta360 X4 and make sure it is ready to connect.
- Open the Insta360 app.
- Launch the Instagram 360 app on your smartphone.
- If you're using the app for the first time, follow the instructions to establish an

account or log in if you already have one.
- Connect with the Camera:
- In the app, tap the camera icon or choose "Connect Camera."
- Follow the on-screen directions to connect your smartphone to the Insta360 X4. This typically entails scanning a QR code displayed on the camera's screen or choosing the camera from a list of accessible devices.
- Once connected, the app will show a live view of the camera and let you adjust its settings.

Firmware Updates

Updating your Insta360 X4 firmware guarantees you have access to the most recent features, upgrades, and bug fixes.

Update the Firmware:

Check for updates.

Launch the Insta360 app on your smartphone.

Ensure that your camera is connected to the app.

Navigate to the app's settings menu and seek the firmware update option.

Download and install:

If an update is available, follow the instructions to download and install it.

Before proceeding with the update, ensure that your camera is fully charged or connected to a power source.

During the update, do not switch off or disconnect your smartphone's camera.

After the update is complete, the camera will restart.

Check the camera or app's settings menu to ensure that the firmware version has been updated.

Manual Firmware Updates:

Download the firmware.

Visit the official Insta360 website to obtain the most recent firmware for the Insta360 X4.

Transfer to a microSD card:

Transfer the firmware file to the root directory of a microSD card.

Insert a microSD card into the camera.

Power on and update:

Turn on the camera and follow the on-screen instructions to install the firmware update.

The camera will immediately detect the firmware file and start the updating process.

To verify the update, restart the camera after completion.

Check the firmware version to see if the upgrade was successful.

By following these instructions, you'll be ready to start capturing great 360-degree content with your Insta360 X4, completely connected and up to date on the latest features and updates.

MASTERING THE CAMERA SETTINGS

1. Resolution and frame rates.

Choosing the Right Resolution

The resolution of your video or photo impacts the amount of detail collected. Higher resolutions provide more detail but require more storage space and computing power. Here's how to select the appropriate resolution for your needs:

Available resolutions for the Insta360 X4:

- 5.7K (5760 x 2880) is the highest resolution available, offering outstanding detail and clarity. Ideal for professional projects, huge screens, and future-proofing content.
- 4K (3840 x 1920) provides a nice blend of detail and file size. Suitable for the majority of

consumer applications, including social networking and YouTube.

- 3K (2880 x 1440): Lower resolution, faster processing, and easier sharing. Ideal for short, casual captures or when storage space is restricted.

Choosing the Right Resolution:

For Professional Use: Select 5.7K to ensure the finest quality and most detail.

For Social Media and Everyday Use: 4K is a versatile option that strikes a balance between quality and functionality.

For quick sharing and limited storage, 3K offers acceptable quality with fewer file sizes.

Understanding frame rates

Frame rate is the number of frames collected per second (fps). Higher frame rates produce smoother motion while significantly increasing file size.

Common frame rates:

- 24 fps: The cinematic standard, which gives your videos a film-like appearance.
- Most video footage uses 30 frames per second, which provides smooth and lifelike action.
- 60 fps is ideal for capturing quick action and generating slow-motion effects.
- 120 fps or higher: Used for super slow motion, which captures incredibly fast movements.

Choosing the Proper Frame Rate:

- Use 24 fps for a conventional, movie-like look.
- For general use, 30 frames per second is excellent for most scenarios since it strikes a reasonable compromise between smoothness and file size.
- For action shots and slow-motion editing, use a frame rate of 60 fps or greater.

2. Shooting modes

Photo modes: Standard, HDR, and Burst.

Standard Mode: For general photography.

Description: Takes a single photo using basic settings. Suitable for most everyday scenarios.

Settings include ISO, shutter speed, and white balance.

HDR Mode: Suitable for high-contrast scenes.

Description: Uses numerous exposures to produce a shot with a wider dynamic range. Suitable for scenarios with both highly brilliant and very dark parts.

Settings: Automatically adjusts for varied exposures.

Use Burst Mode to capture fast-paced action.

Description: Takes a series of photographs in rapid succession.

Perfect for capturing moving subjects.

Settings: Determine the number of images in each burst and the interval between shots.

Video modes: Standard, HDR, and Timelapse.

Standard Mode: For general videography.

Description: Use regular settings to record continuous video. Suitable for most scenarios.

Settings include resolution and frame rate adjustments.

Use HDR Mode for high-contrast video sequences.

Description: Captures video with a wider dynamic range, keeping details in both highlights and shade.

Settings: Automatically optimizes dynamic range.

Timelapse Mode captures changes over time.

Description: When a sequence of frames is recorded at predetermined intervals, it produces a fast-forward effect.

Perfect for demonstrating the passage of time.

Settings include the interval between shots and the duration of the timelapse.

Special modes: bullet time, star-lapse.

Bullet Time Mode creates stunning slow-motion effects.

Captures video at extremely high frame rates as the camera moves in a circular route around the subject. Creates a Matrix-style effect.

Settings: To ensure smooth movement, a specific Bullet Time attachment is required.

Starlapse Mode is used to capture time-lapse images of the night sky.

Description: Takes long-exposure shots at regular intervals to capture the movement of stars in the sky. Ideal for astronomical photography.

Settings: Determine the exposure time, interval, and duration. Use a tripod to keep the camera stable.

Mastering these settings and shooting modes will allow you to create gorgeous, high-quality 360-degree content with your Insta360 X4. Experiment with different combinations to see what best suits your demands and creative vision.

ADVANCED CAMERA SETTINGS

Manual controls: ISO, shutter speed, and white balance.

Understanding and mastering manual controls can greatly improve the quality of your photographs and movies. Here's a full instruction for using these settings on your Insta360 X4:

ISO

What is ISO? ISO measures the camera's sensor's sensitivity to light. A lower ISO value indicates less sensitivity, which reduces noise (graininess), whereas a higher ISO increases sensitivity but may add more noise.

When to Use:

Low ISO (100-400): Use in bright light to obtain clean, sharp photos.

Medium ISO (400-800): Ideal for indoor or shaded environments with moderate lighting.

High ISO (800+): Use in low-light situations, but be mindful of potential noise.

To adjust ISO, use the Insta360 app or touchscreen to access the camera settings menu.

Navigate to the ISO settings and choose an appropriate value according to the lighting circumstances.

Shutter Speed:

What is shutter speed? The shutter speed controls how long the camera's sensor is exposed to light. A quicker shutter speed captures less light and freezes motion, whereas a slower shutter speed permits more light and causes motion blur.

When to Use:

Fast Shutter Speed (1/500 - 1/2000 seconds): Perfect for freezing fast-moving subjects or getting clear shots in bright light.

Medium shutter speed (1/60 to 1/250 seconds): Ideal for general photography with moderate movement.

Slow Shutter Speed (1/60 second or slower): Ideal for low-light photography or creating creative motion blur effects.

To adjust the shutter speed, navigate to the camera settings menu using the touchscreen or the Insta360 app.

Navigate to the shutter speed options and choose the best speed for your scenario.

What is White Balance? White balance corrects the color temperature of your photographs to guarantee accurate color reproduction. To retain true-to-life colors under varying lighting circumstances, multiple white balance settings are required.

When to Use:

Automatic White Balance: The camera changes the white balance based on the scene. Suitable for the majority of scenarios.

Preset Modes: Select from presets such as daylight, cloudy, tungsten, and fluorescent to adapt your lighting circumstances.

Custom White Balance: For fine control, manually adjust the white balance by providing the color temperature (measured in Kelvin).

To adjust the white balance, navigate to the camera settings menu using the touchscreen or the Insta360 app.

Navigate to the white balance settings and select auto, a preset mode, or manually adjust the color temperature.

USING PRESETS FOR QUICK ACCESS

Presets enable you to save and rapidly apply a set of settings for various shooting conditions, making it quicker to transition between setups without manually adjusting each parameter.

Creating and Using Presets

Create a preset:

- Configure your camera with the desired parameters (resolution, frame rate, ISO, shutter speed, and white balance).
- You may access the presets menu using either the touchscreen or the Insta360 app.
- Choose "Create New Preset" and give it a name that describes its purpose (for example, "Low Light," "Action Shots," "Outdoor Daylight").
- Save the preset for later use.

Apply a preset:

- You may access the presets menu using either the touchscreen or the Insta360 app.
- Browse your saved presets and choose the one you wish to use.
- The camera will automatically adjust to the settings stored in the preset.
- To update or delete presets, navigate to the presets menu, select the desired preset, and alter the settings as needed. Save your changes.

- To delete a preset, go to the presets menu, choose the preset you want to remove, and then choose the delete option.

Advantages of using presets:

Efficiency: Quickly switch between different photography configurations without having to manually tweak each option.

Consistency: Use consistent settings for different sorts of shots to ensure uniform quality throughout your movie.

Convenience: Easily adapt to changing conditions by using pre-configured settings tailored to different situations.

By mastering these advanced settings and using presets, you can get complete control over your Insta360 X4, guaranteeing that you shoot the greatest footage possible in any situation. Experiment with different combinations and settings to see what best suits your artistic vision.

CHAPTER THREE

CAPTURING STUNNING 360 PHOTOS AND VIDEOS

1. Photographic Tips

Framing and Composition

Capturing amazing 360 photographs and films necessitates a different approach to framing and composition than traditional photography. Here are some suggestions to help you make the most of the 360-degree format.

Embrace the environment.

Center of Interest: Place the main topic in the middle of the frame to make it the focus of the 360-degree image or movie.

Foreground and background: Take note of both foreground and background elements, as everything in the 360-degree perspective will be visible. Use fascinating foreground items to provide depth and context to your photographs.

Leading lines and symmetry:

Leading lines: Use natural lines in your environment (such as roads, walkways, and rivers) to direct the viewer's attention to the main subject.

Symmetry may produce a balanced and appealing visual impression in 360-degree multimedia. Look for symmetry in architecture, nature, and other settings.

Height and angles:

Height: Experiment with various camera heights to find the most appealing angle. Shooting from a lower angle, for example, might increase the sense of immersion in the situation.

Angle: Avoid putting the camera too close to huge objects or walls, which might cause distortion. Instead, place the camera in an open area to get a more balanced shot.

Movement:

Dynamic Shots: Add movement to your 360 videos by walking or moving the camera slowly. This adds vitality to your footage and keeps the viewer interested.

Stabilization: Use a tripod or stabilizer to keep the camera steady when taking stationary shots. This prevents shaky footage and provides a smooth viewing experience.

USING HDR FOR BETTER PHOTOS

High Dynamic Range (HDR) photography captures a wider range of light and color, resulting in more vibrant and detailed images

Here's how to use HDR efficiently with the Insta360 X4:

Activate HDR mode:

You may access the shooting modes on the camera's touchscreen or through the Insta360 app.

SELECT HDR MODE FOR PHOTOS.

HDR mode automatically snaps multiple exposures of a scene at varying brightness levels.

The camera combines numerous exposures to produce a single image with increased dynamic range, retaining detail in both highlights and shadows.

Tips for using HDR:

Use a Tripod: To eliminate ghosting and ensure that repeated exposures are aligned, use a tripod or hold the camera as motionless as possible.

Static situations: HDR is best used for static situations with little movement. Avoid utilizing HDR while photographing fast-moving subjects or dynamic surroundings.

Lighting Conditions: HDR works best in high-contrast lighting, such as backlit images or landscapes with bright skies and dark foregrounds.

BEST PRACTICES FOR LOW-LIGHT PHOTOGRAPHY

Capturing great 360 photographs and films in low light can be difficult, but the following best practices will help you obtain better results:

Increase ISO sensitivity:

Higher ISO: In low-light situations, boost the ISO setting to make the camera sensor more sensitive to light. Be careful not to set the ISO too high, as this can cause noise.

Manual ISO: Use manual ISO settings to gain more control over your exposure. Begin with a moderate ISO (e.g., 800) and modify as needed according to the lighting circumstances.

Slow Shutter Speed:

Longer exposure: Use a slower shutter speed to let more light into the sensor. This is especially beneficial for photographing night scenes or indoor locations with restricted lighting.

Stabilize the camera. Use a tripod to keep the camera steady during lengthy exposures and avoid motion blur.

Use additional lighting:

External Lighting: Use portable LED lights or other external lighting sources to illuminate the environment. Position the lights to avoid strong shadows and create even lighting.

Built-in Flash: If your camera has a built-in flash, use it carefully to prevent overexposure and harsh illumination. If required, adjust the flash settings to lessen its intensity.

Post-Processing Enhancements:

Noise Reduction: Use post-processing tools to remove noise and improve image quality. The Insta360 app and other editing tools include noise-reduction features for improving low-light photographs.

modify Exposure: In post-processing, modify the exposure, brightness, and contrast to bring out details and make the image more visually attractive.

Following these photography strategies will allow you to produce outstanding 360-degree photographs and films that stand out regardless of the lighting or setting. Experiment with different approaches and settings to see what best suits your artistic vision.

VIDEOGRAPHY TIPS

Smooth panning and tilting.

Smooth panning and tilting are critical skills for producing compelling, professional-looking 360 videos. Here's how to accomplish them:

Use a gimbal or stabilizer.

Invest in a high-quality gimbal specifically designed for 360 cameras. A gimbal stabilizes the camera, eliminating shaking and vibrations while allowing for smooth panning and tilting movements.

Stabilizer: For smoother motions, utilize a handheld stabilizer or tripod with a fluid head.

Move slowly and steadily.

Slow Movements: To avoid choppy footage, pan and tilt the camera gently and steadily. Rapid motions can be distracting to viewers and result in poor video quality.

Practice: Improve your panning and tilting skills to achieve constant, smooth movements. Before taping, plan your shots and rehearse the actions.

Use the Insta360 app:

Remote Control: With the Insta360 app, you can remotely control the camera and perform seamless panning and tilting movements. The app gives you precise control over the camera's movements, allowing for more polished photos.

Preview Mode: The app's preview mode allows you to see how the panning and tilting will appear in the final video. To obtain the desired effect, adjust the speed and direction accordingly. Using Bullet Time for Dramatic Effects

Bullet Time is a special shooting mode that creates a dramatic slow-motion effect, capturing high-speed movements uniquely and engagingly. Here's how to use Bullet Time with your Insta360 X4:

Set Up the Bullet Time Accessory:

Accessory: Use the Bullet Time handle or selfie stick specifically developed for the Insta360 X4.

These accessories let you swing the camera around in a circular motion.

Attach the Camera: Securely connect the Insta360 X4 to the Bullet Time attachment.

Activate Bullet Time Mode.

Select mode: You may access the shooting modes on the camera's touchscreen or through the Insta360 app.

Bullet Time: Select the Bullet Time mode. The camera will

automatically adjust the settings for the best slow-motion capture.

Capture the shot.

Swing the camera: Hold the Bullet Time handle or selfie stick and swing the camera in a smooth, circular motion around yourself. Make sure the movement is uniform and at a steady pace.

Maintain Distance: Keep the camera at a consistent distance from your body for a smooth and even effect.

Bullet time footage editing and enhancements:

Insta360 App: Use the Insta360 app to edit Bullet Time footage. The program includes features for fine-tuning the pace, adding effects, and improving the overall quality of the video.

Experiment with various angles and heights to create unique and dramatic Bullet Time shots.

Creating seamless timelapse

Timelapse films compress large amounts of time into brief,

fascinating scenes. Here's how to create seamless time-lapses using your Insta360 X4:

Select Timelapse mode:

Access the shooting modes via the camera's touchscreen or the Insta360 app.

Timelapse: Select the Timelapse mode. The camera will automatically change the settings for the best timelapse capture.

Set the interval and duration.

Interval: Select the time between shots (for example, 1 second, 5 seconds, or 10 seconds). Shorter intervals result in smoother time lapses, whereas longer intervals record more dramatic shifts.

period: Determine the overall period of the timelapse (for example, 10 minutes or 1 hour). The duration indicates how long the camera will continue to capture photographs.

Stabilize the camera.

Tripod: Use a tripod to hold the camera stable throughout the timelapse. This results in smooth, consistent footage.

Fixed location: Keep the camera in a fixed location to prevent movement or shifts that could break the timelapse.

Capture the scene.

Press Record: Begin the timelapse recording by pushing the shutter button or opening the Insta360 app.

Monitor Progress: Keep an eye on the camera to ensure it continues to record without interruption. If you are shooting a long timelapse, make sure the battery is fully charged or linked to an external power source.

Editing and enhancements:

Insta360 Application: Use the Insta360 app to edit your timelapse clip. The program lets you change the tempo, add music, and apply effects to improve the final movie.

Smooth Transitions: To ensure smooth transitions between frames, use the app's stabilization capabilities. This helps to generate a smooth and visually appealing timelapse.

Following these videography guidelines will allow you to make gorgeous, professional-quality 360 videos with your Insta360 X4. Experiment with various techniques and settings to see what works best for your creative projects and produces the desired results.

EDITING AND POST-PROCESSING

Using the Insta360 App

The Insta360 app is a powerful tool for importing, organizing, and editing your 360-degree footage. Here's how to make the most of it:

IMPORTING AND ORGANIZING FOOTAGE

To import footage, first connect your Insta360 X4 camera to your smartphone using Wi-Fi or Bluetooth.

Launch the Insta360 app on your smartphone.

Import Media:

Navigate to the "Album" section of the app.

Tap the import option, then select the film you wish to transfer from your camera to your smartphone.

The software will import the selected files, making them available for editing and sharing.

Organizing footage:

Create albums:

The app's album function allows you to create and name albums for various projects or events.

Move your imported film to these albums for easier organizing and access.

Tag your photographs and videos with keywords or labels to easily discover specific content.

Use the app's search feature to find marked content.

Delete unnecessary clips from the app to save up storage space and organize your collection.

CHAPTER FOUR

BASIC EDITING TOOLS AND TECHNIQUES

The Insta360 app has a variety of basic editing features that are simple to use, even for beginners. Here's a look at some of the important features:

Trim & Cut:

- To edit footage, select Clip and open it in the app.
- Use the trim tool to select the beginning and finish points of

your clip, deleting any unnecessary areas.
- To edit longer videos, use the cut tool to eliminate certain chunks.

Adjustments:

- Adjust the exposure and brightness of your footage using the tools provided.
- Brightness can be increased for dark scenes or reduced for extremely bright films.
- Adjust contrast and saturation to highlight the difference between light and dark parts.

- Change the saturation to make colors more vibrant, or tone them down for a more muted appearance.

Speed Control:

- For slow-motion and time-lapse videos, alter the playback speed using the speed control tool.
- Create slow-motion effects by decreasing the speed or time-lapse effects by increasing it.

Stabilization:

Use Insta360's FlowState stabilization to improve shaky

footage and create a more professional appearance.

ADDING EFFECTS AND MUSIC

Adding Effects:

Filters: Customize the appearance and feel of your film using a range of filters.

Apply filters to your video to get a specific mood or creative impact.

Use transition effects to create smooth transitions between clips.

Choose from various transition styles, including fades, wipes, and dissolves.

Use text overlays and titles to add context and enhance your movie.

Adjust the font, size, color, and location of your text.

To add background music to your movie, use the app's built-in music library.

Choose tracks that suit the atmosphere and tone of your footage.

You can import your music files into the app.

Make sure you have the right to utilize any imported music in your films.

To sync music with your video, adjust its time to match critical points.

Using the app's editing tools, cut and change the length of the music track to match the footage.

Finalization and Export:

Review your edited video to confirm all changes and additions are as intended.

Make any last revisions as necessary.

Export Settings: Select the appropriate video resolution and format.

Export the finished video to your smartphone's gallery or share it straight on social networking networks from within the app.

USING INSTA360 STUDIO ON DESKTOP

Insta360 Studio is a robust desktop application that offers comprehensive editing options for 360-degree videos. Here's how to make the best of it:

Installation & setup:

Download and install:

Visit the official Insta360 website and get Insta360 Studio for your operating system (Windows or macOS).

Install the software according to the on-screen directions.

Importing footage:

Connect your Insta360 X4 to your computer via a USB connection, or plug the microSD card directly into your computer.

To upload your footage to the workspace, open Insta360 Studio and click "Import".

Editing Tools:

Use the toolbar to make simple edits to your footage, including trimming, chopping, and cropping.

To improve the visual quality of your movies, adjust the exposure, contrast, and color balance settings.

Apply FlowState Stabilization to smooth out unstable footage and produce a professional appearance.

Adjust the stabilization settings to match the amount of movement in your footage.

Keyframes help generate smooth camera movements in 360 videos. Set keyframes at various positions to control panning, tilting, and zooming.

This allows you to focus the viewer's attention on select parts of the video.

Reframing: Use the tools to generate flat films from 360 footage. Choose specific angles and perspectives to emphasize critical moments.

Export these reframed videos in conventional video formats for use on systems that do not support 360-degree content.

Adjust your video's playback speed to generate slow-motion or time-lapse effects.

The speed ramping tool allows you to effortlessly transition between several speeds within a single clip.

Apply lens correction to reduce distortion and get a more realistic image when using specific camera accessories or mounts.

Exporting footage:

Select the appropriate resolution, format, and bitrate for your exported video. MP4 and MOV are common file formats.

Adjust the export options to balance quality and file size according to your requirements.

Batch export allows you to process numerous clips at once, saving time and effort.

STITCHING AND EXPORTING 360 VIDEOS

Insta360 Studio seamlessly merges footage from the camera's two lenses into a seamless 360-degree video.

Check the stitched video to make sure there are no noticeable seams or distortions.

Manually adjust stitching to correct alignment difficulties.

Use Insta360 Studio's stitching calibration tools to fine-tune the footage's overlap and alignment.

Exporting 360 Videos:

Select a suitable export format for your 360 video. Common projection formats include equirectangular and fisheye.

Use the equirectangular format on networks such as YouTube and Facebook.

Select the resolution and bitrate for your exported video. Higher resolutions and bitrates improve quality but result in higher file sizes.

The most common 360 video resolutions are 4K, 5.7K, and 8K.

Metadata Injection:

Make sure your video has the proper information to be identified as a 360-degree video by platforms such as YouTube and Facebook.

Insta360 Studio usually handles this automatically, but you can check the settings before exporting.

To export your video, click the "Export" button and select the desired destination folder.

Monitor the export process and inspect the finished product to verify it satisfies your quality standards.

ENHANCING PHOTOS WITH EXTERNAL SOFTWARE

While Insta360 Studio provides robust editing tools, you can further enhance your photos using external software like Adobe Photoshop, Lightroom, or GIMP. Here's how to integrate these tools into your workflow:

Exporting Photos for External Editing:

Export 360 photographs from Insta360 Studio in high-quality formats like TIFF or JPEG.

If you intend to save the exported files as 360-degree photographs, make sure they contain the 360 information.

Open in external software.

Open the exported photo using your choice of photo editing software.

Editing techniques:

- Adjust your photo's exposure, contrast, and color balance to enhance its overall appearance.
- Use curves and level adjustments to have more exact

control over shadows, mid-tones, and highlights.
- Apply noise reduction techniques to remove graininess, especially in low-light images.
- Use selective noise reduction to preserve information in essential areas while minimizing background noise.
- Enhance your photo's sharpness and clarity to highlight details.
- To get the necessary amount of detail, use tools such as unsharp

masking and clarity adjustments.

- Retouching: Use cloning and healing techniques to remove undesired items or imperfections from photos.
- Make selective edits to improve specific areas, such as lightening the subject or incorporating a vignette to draw attention.
- Saving and exporting enhanced photographs:
- Save your altered photos in high-quality format, including any 360 metadata.

For classic flat photos, use a standard format such as JPEG or PNG.

To view or share a modified 360 photo in Insta360 Studio, simply re-import it.

Check that the 360-degree view and metadata are intact.

SHARING YOUR CREATIONS

Social Media Integration

Sharing your 360-degree photographs and movies on social media allows you to reach a larger audience while also showcasing your talent. Here's how to upload directly to popular platforms and create compelling content.

Uploading directly to Instagram, Facebook, and YouTube

Export and transfer your altered 360 content from Insta360 Studio or the app in a compatible format (e.g., MP4 for films, and JPEG for images).

If the file does not already exist on your smartphone, transfer it there.

To open Instagram, launch the app on your smartphone.

- Because Instagram does not natively enable complete 360-degree viewing, you may need to convert your 360 photographs to Tiny Planet or Pano format.
- To upload content, tap the "+" button to make a new post.
- Select a photo or video from your gallery.
- Adjust and add filters or captions as needed.

- Tap "Share" to add the content to your Instagram feed.

For Facebook, export and transfer 360 content from Insta360 Studio or the app in a suitable format, retaining all relevant metadata.

- To access Facebook, either open the app or use your web browser.
- Navigate to the profile or page where you intend to upload the content.
- To upload content, select "Photo/Video" while creating a new post.

- Select a 360 photo or video from your device.
- Facebook should automatically identify the 360 format and present it appropriately.
- To share your content, include a caption and any tags, then click "Post".
- Export and transfer 360 videos from Insta360 Studio to YouTube in MP4 format with 360 metadata.
- **To access YouTube,** either use the app or use your web browser.

- Go to your channel and click the camera icon to upload a video.
- To upload content, select the 360 video file from your smartphone.
- Enter the video's title, description, and tags.
- Make sure the "360 video" option is chosen in the video settings.
- Click "Publish" to upload your 360-degree video to YouTube.

TIPS FOR ENGAGING CONTENT

High-quality content:

quality: Always upload at the greatest quality available to guarantee that your content seems sharp and professional.

Lighting: Proper lighting can significantly improve the quality of your 360 photographs and films.

Interactivity:

Encourage viewers to interact with your 360 material by using captions like "Swipe around to explore" or "Move your device to see more."

Annotations: Use annotations or text overlays to direct viewers to specific points of interest in your 360 material.

Storytelling:

Engaging Narrative: Create a narrative or story that will keep viewers interested. Consider how the 360-degree perspective might improve your storytelling.

Similar themes: To create a recognizable brand, keep your posts similar in theme or design.

Frequency and timing:

Regular Posts: To keep your audience engaged, post regularly.

Optimal Timing: Post when your audience is most active to boost engagement.

VIRTUAL REALITY

Virtual Reality (VR) enhances the immersive experience provided by 360-degree material. Here's how you may see your 360 content in

VR and share your experiences with peers.

VIEWING YOUR 360 CONTENT IN VR

Compatible VR headsets:

Make sure your VR headset is compatible with 360-degree content. Popular options include the Oculus Rift, Oculus Quest, HTC Vive, and Google Cardboard.

Transfer 360 photographs and videos to your virtual reality headset. This can be accomplished via USB, microSD card, or wireless transfer, depending on the headset.

Open the VR Player:

To view your 360 content, use the built-in media player on your VR headset or a third-party VR media player app.

Select a 360 photo or video for an immersive viewing experience.

Smartphone VR Apps:

Install a VR-watching app for your smartphone, such as YouTube VR, Facebook 360, or a standalone VR media player.

Insert into the VR Headset:

Insert your smartphone into a compatible VR headset, such as Google Cardboard or Samsung Gear VR.

To view 360 content in VR mode, open the VR app and select the desired content.

SHARING VR EXPERIENCES WITH FRIENDS

Social Media VR Sharing:

To use YouTube VR, upload your 360 videos and share the URL with your friends. They can watch the content in VR with the YouTube VR app and a suitable headset.

Share 360 photographs and videos on Facebook. Friends with VR headsets can view your content in immersive VR mode right from their news feed.

VR Platforms and Applications:

Oculus Venues allows you to hold virtual events and share 360 content with a bigger audience in a social VR environment.

VR Chat: Use apps like VRChat or AltspaceVR to share 360-degree content in virtual chat rooms or gatherings. This allows friends to view your material in a shared virtual world.

Direct Sharing:

Share your 360 photographs and videos with friends via a USB drive or online storage services such as Google Drive or Dropbox.

They can download the content and watch it with their own VR headsets.

In-Person VR watching: Invite pals for a watching session. Set up your VR headset and allow them to see your 360 material firsthand.

You may use social media integration with virtual reality to share your 360 projects with a larger audience and provide immersive experiences that attract and engage them. Experiment with various platforms and sharing techniques to determine which works best for your content and audience.

CHAPTER FIVE

ACCESSORIES AND ENHANCEMENTS

1. Essential Accessories

To get the most out of your Insta360 X4, consider investing in some essential accessories. These will enhance your shooting experience and help protect your equipment.

RECOMMENDED TRIPODS AND MOUNTS

Tripods:

Manfrotto Compact Action Tripod is lightweight and compact, making it ideal for taking stable 360-degree photos.

The joystick head allows for easy adjustments and smooth panning.

Joby GorillaPod 5K features flexible legs that wrap around objects for versatile mounting choices.

Strong enough to hold the Insta360 X4 firmly.

Mounts:

Insta360 Selfie Stick is an extendable selfie stick made for 360 cameras.

Invisible in shots, creating the sense of a floating camera.

The Insta360 Bullet Time Handle is specifically built for Bullet Time shots.

Allows you to move the camera in a smooth, circular manner.

Suction Cup Mount: Insta360 Suction Cup Mount attaches to flat surfaces, such as automobile windows or dashboards.

Ideal for filming dynamic 360 footage while on the move.

Chest and helmet mounts:

The Insta360 Chest Strap Mount offers a first-person perspective by placing the camera on your chest.

Suitable for adrenaline sports and hands-free shooting.

Helmet Mount: Attaches securely to helmets for immersive POV shots when bicycling or skiing.

Protective Cases:

The Insta360 Hard Shell Case is durable and water-resistant, protecting your camera and accessories.

Customizable foam inserts for securing the camera and other equipment.

The Insta360 Soft Carry Case is compact and lightweight, ideal for daily usage and travel.

Offers basic protection against scratches and moderate impacts.

Lens Protectors:

Insta360 Lens Guards are snap-on guards that shield camera lenses from scratches and dust.

Simple to attach and remove, preserving the quality of your lenses.

The Insta360 Dive Case is a waterproof enclosure suitable for underwater shooting up to 30 meters.

It protects the camera while allowing for complete 360-degree filming underwater.

ENHANCING YOUR EXPERIENCE YOUR 360 EXPERIENCE

To further enhance your 360-degree shooting experience, consider using external microphones and exploring additional lenses and filters.

USING EXTERNAL MICROPHONES

Benefits:

Improved Audio Quality: External microphones produce greater sound quality than built-in microphones, particularly in noisy circumstances.

Directional Sound: Some external microphones may collect directional sound, which focuses on specific audio sources while decreasing background noise.

Recommended microphones:

Rode VideoMicro is compact and lightweight, making it ideal for mobile recording.

Includes a shock mount and windscreen to reduce handling noise and wind interference.

Zoom H1n Handy Recorder is a portable audio recorder that captures high-quality stereo sound.

Can be mounted on the camera or used independently for increased versatility.

Connecting microphones:

Use a TRS to TRRS adapter cable to attach external microphones to the Insta360 X4.

Check compatibility with your microphone and camera setup.

Consider cordless microphone systems, such as the Rode cordless GO, for increased mobility.

EXPLORING ADDITIONAL LENSES AND FILTERS

Benefits:

Creative Effects: Using additional lenses and filters can offer distinctive visual effects and improve the quality of your footage.

Versatility: Increase the number of shooting settings by adjusting to diverse lighting conditions and environments.

Recommended lenses:

Insta360 Farsight is an extended lens system that expands the field of view and enhances the immersive experience.

Ideal for photographing big landscapes and massive scenes.

FILTERS:

Neutral Density (ND) filters limit light entering the lens, providing better exposure control in bright conditions.

Useful for creating motion blur effects and ensuring adequate exposure during lengthy exposures, especially in bright sunlight.

Polarizing filters improve footage's color and contrast by reducing reflections and glare.

Suitable for shooting near water, snow, or glass surfaces.

UV filters protect camera lenses from UV rays and physical damage.

Helpful for eliminating haze and increasing overall image clarity.

Using filters:

Before attaching filters, ensure they are compatible with your camera and lens combination.

Attach the filters tightly and inspect for vignetting or image distortion.

Experiment with combining filters to obtain desired effects. For example, in bright outdoor circumstances, use both ND and polarizing filters.

By combining these extras and modifications into your filming setup, you may greatly improve the quality and versatility of your 360-degree footage. Experiment with different combinations to see what best suits your creative vision and photography demands.

TROUBLESHOOTING AND MAINTENANCE

COMMON ISSUES AND SOLUTIONS

CONNECTIVITY PROBLEMS

Issue: Unable to connect the camera to the smartphone via Wi-Fi or Bluetooth.

Solutions:

Check camera and smartphone settings to ensure Wi-Fi and Bluetooth are enabled.

Check that the camera is in pairing mode and visible on your smartphone.

To reset connections, turn off the smartphone's camera, Wi-Fi, and Bluetooth and then turn them back on.

Repair your smartphone after forgetting the camera in its Bluetooth settings.

Update the firmware and app:

Ensure that both the camera's firmware and the Insta360 app are up to date. Updates frequently contain bug fixes and better connectivity features.

Reboot the Devices:

Restart both the camera and the smartphone. This often resolves temporary connectivity concerns.

To increase connection quality, avoid interference from other wireless devices.

Issue: Slow or unstable Wi-Fi connection. Solutions:

Close unneeded background apps to free up smartphone resources.

Proximity: Keep the camera and smartphone within 1-2 meters.

Reset your smartphone's network settings. Please keep in mind that this will delete all previously saved Wi-Fi networks and Bluetooth pairings.

To improve Wi-Fi stability and speed, consider switching to a 5GHz band (if supported).

SOFTWARE GLITCHES AND FIXES

Issue: Camera freezes or becomes unresponsive.

Solutions:

To restart the camera, first, turn it off and remove the battery. Wait a few seconds before reinserting the battery and turning the camera back on.

To reset the camera, navigate to the settings menu and select factory reset. It should be noted that this will wipe all camera settings and data.

Check for and install the most recent firmware update. Firmware updates can fix a variety of software issues.

Issue: The app crashes or fails to load.

Solutions:

Update the App:

Make sure the Insta360 app has been updated to the newest version.

To reinstall the Insta360 app, first uninstall it from your smartphone.

To remove the app cache and data on your smartphone, navigate to Settings > Apps > Insta360.

Check Compatibility: Ensure your smartphone satisfies the minimal system requirements for the Insta360 app.

Issue: Footage appears distorted or improperly stitched.

Solutions:

Use the lens calibration option in Insta360 Studio or the app to fix stitching issues.

When mounting the camera, keep it away from heavy objects or shiny surfaces to ensure accurate placement.

Manually tweak stitching settings in Insta360 Studio for optimal results.

MAINTAINING YOUR CAMERA

Cleaning and Care Tips

Lens Care:

To clean the lenses, gently wipe them with a soft, lint-free cloth.

Avoid abrasive items that may scratch the lens.

To remove stubborn smudges, use a lens cleaning solution and a microfiber cloth.

Use lens covers to avoid scratches and damage. Replace them if they get scratched or damaged.

Body Care:

Dust and debris:

Remove dust and debris from the camera body with a soft brush or compressed air, paying careful attention to the buttons and ports.

Waterproof Before exposing the camera to water, ensure all seals are intact and closed properly. Check for signs of wear and tear regularly.

Battery Care:

Charging: Use the included cord and charger. Avoid using third-party chargers, since they may not be compatible.

Don't overload the battery. Disconnect it once it has been fully charged.

Store the batteries in a cool, dry area. Do not expose it to harsh temperatures.

General Care: Store the camera in a protective case while not in use to prevent physical harm.

Store the camera in a dry, dust-free area.

Handle the camera carefully, especially when attaching or removing accessories.

ENSURING LONGEVITY OF YOUR INSTA360 X4

Regular updates:

Firmware: Update the camera's firmware to take advantage of the most recent features and upgrades.

App: Regularly update the Insta360 app to ensure compatibility and access to new features.

Proper Usage:

Operating Conditions: Keep the camera within the prescribed temperature and humidity levels.

Avoid Overuse: To avoid overheating, let the camera cool down between extended recording sessions.

Maintenance:

Check seals: Inspect watertight seals regularly and replace any that show indications of deterioration.

Service: If the camera develops problems that cannot be solved through troubleshooting, contact expert assistance from Insta360 or an authorized service center.

By following these troubleshooting and maintenance instructions, you can keep your Insta360 X4 in peak condition, offering dependable performance for all of your 360-degree photography and videography needs.

EXPERT GUIDE ON USING THE INSTA360 X4 FOR RIDES

For some years now, I've been documenting my motorbike rides, bicycle excursions, and other activities with Insta360 cameras. If you're not familiar with them, believe me when I say they represent a major development in the field of photo and video capturing technology. Particularly for fans of motorsports, these cameras are an amazing deal of fun. I got to test out the X4, the newest high-spec consumer camera from Insta360, recently.

ANNOUNCING THE INSTA360 X4

About the size of a candy bar, the Insta360 X4 camera offers 360-degree capture in addition to all the features of a phone camera. Using advanced software, "360-

degree cameras" fuse photos taken by twin fisheye lenses on either side of the camera to record in all directions. The end effect is images and films that, when played back, let viewers explore in any direction inside a "sphere". Using their mouse, trackpad, phone, tablet, or laptop screen, viewers can move through the film, enlarging and contracting to obtain various viewpoints.

CHAPTER SIX

RECORDING AND SHARING YOUR RIDE

I usually attach the camera on the bike using a clip that has a little foldable pole to provide some distance from the subject when I record a ride. Some users affix the camera to a chest or helmet mount. With an optional dive case, the waterproof Insta360 X4 (and its predecessor, the X3) can be used deeper than snorkeling depths. They also work as a typical

4K still or video camera, webcam, action camera, or dashcam.

The true brilliance of the Insta360's technology is its 360-degree capabilities, which lets viewers "look around" during video playback, therefore transporting them back to the moment the video was shot. In a cathedral, for example, you can gaze up at the vaulted ceiling as well as in every other direction. Although 360-degree cameras require plenty of light to function optimally, the results are nonetheless remarkable in low light.

Specifications and capabilities of the insta 360 X4

The entire 8K resolution of the new X4 gives exported films and stills even better quality than the 5.7K of the previous generation. Higher frame rates made feasible by lower resolutions enable for editing effects of slow motion. Very versatile, the camera also offers time-lapse, dashcam, "bullet time," and long-exposure night sky photo modes.

Numerous in-built microphones on the X4 have strong wind noise reduction capabilities. It can be remotely controlled by speech, hand motions, or smartphone and can connect with Bluetooth headsets for improved narration. Videos are kept smooth by motion stabilization technology, and setup changes and speedy playback are made possible by the tiny color touchscreen.

Editing and posting

Quick publishing and basic yet powerful editing are features of the Insta360 smartphone app. Further accurate editing in Adobe Premiere or Final Cut Pro is also made possible by plugins. Viewer controls are added by YouTube automatically when a 360-degree movie is uploaded. Still, because 8K resolution has such high requirements, a computer and monitor are advised for best viewing.

For virtual reality headsets like the Oculus Quest and Apple Vision Pro, the 360-degree format works flawlessly, however, there are still compatibility problems. An almost science fiction degree of immersion into the recorded events will be possible with the 8K resolution once they are fixed.

SHOOTING TIPS FOR EVERY SCENARIO

These are the essentials for 360º videos. Now, here are some pro tips for each scenario. Skip ahead to the one that interests you, or read them all if you're a multi-talented person!

TRAVEL AND CREATIVE VIDEOGRAPHY

Capture the excitement at its peak with Matrix-level slow-motion—Bullet Time now runs at 5.7K120fps! This is a wonderful shot for couples looking to add drama to their videos, especially if shot in multiple locations and put together.

To use Bullet Time with Insta360 X4, attach the selfie stick to the handle, select Bullet Time Mode, then swing it overhead at a rate of 1 second each 360º spin. To achieve the greatest results, keep one lens up and one down!

If slow-motion isn't your thing, try accelerating time with this spectacular 11K Timelapse! The 5nm AI Chip creates timelapse videos from 72MP PureShot images, delivering more detail and clarity than ever before. It's perfect for showcasing a new city or a sunset over the mountains.

Tip: Are you worried about missing your early morning alarm? Set Timed Capture and the X4 will turn on, shoot, store the file, and shut off automatically, assuring you never miss a sunrise again.

With 8K TimeShifts, you may capture cinematic images without devoting an hour to your workflow! They're pleasant and straightforward to make, with a wide range of camera movements to choose from during the editing process. You can appear to travel through time and space (while strolling with the Invisible Selfie Stick).

Prepare to ride the X4 motorcycle! It is compatible with leading helmet headsets from Sena and Cardo and has Auto Dash, Loop

Recording, and Gesture Control for easy filming.

There are several accessories available to mount your X4 in whatever configuration you can envision. The Motorcycle U-Bolt Mount is vital for getting sharp third-person shots and outrageous angles. The Chest Strap enables you to capture excellent aboard shots, while the Helmet Mount Kit opens your rider's eye. If you only require the most essentials, the X4 Motorcycle Bundle has you covered.

BIKING

The X4 is great for bikers, whether on trails or false flats. You can add stats from your Garmin device or Apple Watch, replace your headset cap with the new Bike Headset Cap Mount, shoot third-person angles with the Third-Person Handlebar Mount or Action Invisible Selfie Stick, and control your camera completely from your wrist with the GPS Preview Remote. The alternatives are unlimited.

Tip: Use the Motion ND effect in the Insta360 app or Studio to produce cinematic cycling shots without an ND filter! It provides a genuine sense of speed as you race down courses and roads.

Underwater light refraction magnifies and distorts pictures, making stitching 360º videos more difficult than on land. So, while the X4 is waterproof to 33 feet (10 meters) straight out of the box, we recommend teaming it with the Invisible Dive Case for any underwater excursion!

WINTER SPORTS

The X4 can resist temperatures as low as -4ºF (-20ºC), making it suitable for snowboarding and skiing. Try shooting in Me Mode: it's a great way to slow down jumps, spins, and shreds for a dramatic impact, but it can also help you improve your technique. With your full body in view, you can easily evaluate your motions (and mistakes!).

DRIVING

Say goodbye to limitations with the Dual/Triple Suction Cup Car Mount, which allows you to take unique third-person driving photos. Mount the X4 with the Action Invisible Selfie Stick for #RealLifeGTA shots that look like they came straight out of a video game! The all-metal suction cup base and carbon fiber support bar are built to withstand shocks and vibrations, so you can drive with confidence.

Use these tips to get the most out of your Insta360 X4 and create stunning 360º videos and photos. Happy shooting!

SNORKELING WITH THE INSTA360 X4

Snorkeling is an incredible way to explore the underwater world, and capturing those experiences with the Insta360 X4 makes it even more memorable. Here's a guide on how to make the most of your Insta360 X4 while snorkeling.

Preparing Your Insta360 X4 for Snorkeling

1. Waterproofing:

Built-in Waterproofing: The Insta360 X4 is waterproof up to 10 meters (33 feet) without any additional housing, making it perfect for snorkeling adventures.

Optional Dive Case: For added protection and deeper dives, consider using the optional dive case. This ensures your camera stays safe from water damage and provides extra durability.

2. Pre-Dive Checks:

Battery and Memory: Ensure your battery is fully charged and that you have ample memory space. Recording in high resolution can quickly fill up storage, so having a high-capacity microSD card is essential.

Lens Cleanliness: Check that the lenses are clean and free of smudges. Use a microfiber cloth to gently clean the lenses if necessary.

Capturing Stunning Underwater Footage

1. Optimal Settings:

Resolution: Set your camera to the highest resolution (8K) for the best video quality. This ensures you capture all the details of the underwater world.

Frame Rate: Choose a higher frame rate (e.g., 60fps) if you plan to slow down the footage in post-processing. This makes your videos smooth and visually appealing.

Stabilization: Ensure FlowState stabilization is enabled to keep your footage steady despite the movement of the water.

2. Mounting Options:

Handheld: Hold the camera or use a floating handle to keep the camera stable and buoyant.

Selfie Stick: Use an extendable selfie stick to get closer to marine life without disturbing them and to capture a wider field of view.

Chest or Head Mount: For hands-free recording, use a chest or head mount. This provides a first-person perspective and allows you to focus on swimming.

3. Shooting Techniques:

Slow Movements: Move the camera slowly and steadily to avoid disturbing the marine environment and to capture smooth, clear footage.

Angles and Perspectives: Experiment with different angles and perspectives. Capture shots from above, below, and at eye level with marine life.

Close-Ups: Get close to interesting subjects like coral reefs, fish, and other marine creatures. Ensure you don't touch or harm the wildlife.

4. Using HDR Mode:

High Dynamic Range (HDR): Use HDR mode to capture better color and contrast in your underwater photos and videos. This mode is particularly useful in environments with varying light conditions, such as the transition between shallow and deeper waters.

Editing and Sharing Your Underwater Adventure

1. Importing Footage:

Transfer Files: Connect your Insta360 X4 to your smartphone or computer to transfer the footage. Use the Insta360 app or Insta360 Studio for desktop importing.

Organize: Organize your clips and photos into folders to make editing easier.

2. Basic Editing:

Trim and Cut: Use the Insta360 app to trim and cut your footage, removing any unwanted sections.

Color Correction: Adjust the color balance to compensate for the blue and green hues that dominate underwater footage. Increase the brightness and contrast to enhance visibility.

Stabilization: Apply additional stabilization if needed to smooth out any shaky footage.

3. Adding Effects and Music:

Effects: Add effects like slow motion or time-lapse to create dynamic and engaging videos.

Music: Incorporate background music to complement your footage. Choose tracks that match the mood of your underwater adventure.

4. Sharing:

Social Media: Share your edited videos and photos on platforms like Instagram, Facebook, and YouTube. Use hashtags like

#Insta360 and #Snorkeling to reach a wider audience.

VR Headsets: For an immersive experience, view your 360-degree videos with VR headsets like Oculus Quest or Apple Vision Pro. Share these experiences with friends to give them a taste of your underwater exploration.

Tips for a Great Snorkeling Experience

1. Respect Marine Life:

No Touching: Avoid touching corals or marine creatures to protect the delicate ecosystem.

Safe Distance: Maintain a safe distance from marine life to prevent causing stress or harm.

2. Safety First:

Buddy System: Always snorkel with a buddy for safety.

Stay Aware: Be aware of your surroundings, including currents, tides, and potential hazards.

3. Capture the Moment:

Stay Relaxed: Enjoy the snorkeling experience and capture the beauty of the underwater world without rushing. The more relaxed you are, the better your footage will be.

CHAPTER SEVEN

HOW TO LIVE STREAM AND APPLY STABILIZATION WITH YOUR INSTA360 X4

The Insta360 X4 is a powerful tool for capturing immersive 360-degree content, and its live streaming and stabilization features allow you to share your experiences in real-time with a smooth, professional look. Here's a detailed guide on how to livestream and apply stabilization with your Insta360 X4.

LIVE STREAMING WITH INSTA360 X4

Step 1: Set Up the Camera and App

Install the Insta360 App:

Ensure you have the latest version of the Insta360 app installed on your smartphone. The app is available on both the App Store (iOS) and Google Play Store (Android).

Connect Your Camera:

Turn on your Insta360 X4.

Open the Insta360 app and connect your camera via Wi-Fi or Bluetooth. Follow the on-screen instructions to pair your devices.

Step 2: Prepare for Live Streaming

Select Live Streaming Mode:

In the Insta360 app, navigate to the shooting modes and select "Live Stream."

Choose a Platform:

The Insta360 X4 supports live streaming to platforms such as YouTube, Facebook, and other RTMP-supported services.

Select your desired platform and log in to your account if prompted.

Configure Streaming Settings:

Resolution and Bitrate: Choose the appropriate resolution and bitrate for your live stream. Higher resolutions provide better quality but require more bandwidth. Common settings are 1080p at 4 Mbps.

Stream URL and Key: If using a custom RTMP service, enter the stream URL and stream key provided by your streaming platform.

Step 3: Start Live Streaming

Position Your Camera:

Mount your Insta360 X4 on a tripod or selfie stick for a stable setup. Ensure it's positioned to capture the desired scene.

Start Streaming:

Tap the "Start Live" button in the app to begin streaming. The app will indicate when the stream is live.

Monitor the Stream:

Use the app to monitor your live stream and interact with viewers. Ensure you have a stable internet connection to maintain the stream quality.

APPLYING STABILIZATION WITH INSTA360 X4

The Insta360 X4's FlowState stabilization ensures your footage is smooth and watchable, even in dynamic conditions. Here's how to apply and enhance stabilization for your recordings.

Step 1: Record with Stabilization Enabled

Enable FlowState Stabilization:

Ensure FlowState stabilization is enabled in your camera settings. This is usually on by default, but you can verify it in the Insta360 app under the settings menu.

Capture Steady Footage:

Hold the camera steady and use a tripod or a gimbal for best results. While FlowState stabilization compensates for movement, minimizing excessive motion will yield the best results.

Step 2: Enhance Stabilization During Editing

Import Footage to Insta360 Studio:

Transfer your recorded footage to your computer and open it in Insta360 Studio, which is available for both Windows and macOS.

Apply Additional Stabilization:

Select your video clip and open the stabilization options.

Apply additional stabilization if necessary by using the advanced settings to fine-tune the stabilization effect.

Keyframing and Editing:

Use keyframes to create smooth transitions and control camera movements within your 360 footage. This helps direct the viewer's attention and enhances the overall viewing experience.

Step 3: Export and Share

Export Stabilized Footage:

After applying stabilization and any other edits, export your video in the desired format and resolution. Insta360 Studio supports various export options to suit different platforms.

Share Your Video:

Upload your stabilized video to your preferred platform, such as YouTube, Facebook, or Vimeo. Ensure that you export in a format compatible with the platform's 360-degree video support.

Tips for Best Results

Stable Mounting: Use a stable mounting solution like a tripod or a chest mount to minimize unnecessary movement during recording.

Lighting Conditions: Ensure good lighting conditions to enhance video quality, as low light can introduce noise and affect stabilization.

Practice Movements: Smooth, controlled movements yield the best stabilization results. Practice your recording techniques to improve overall video quality.

HOW TO USE THE INVISIBLE SELFIE STICK FEATURE ON YOUR INSTA360 X4

The invisible selfie stick is one of the standout features of the Insta360 X4, allowing you to capture immersive 360-degree footage without the stick appearing in your shots. This guide will explain how to use the invisible selfie stick and when to make the most of this feature.

SETTING UP THE INVISIBLE SELFIE STICK

Step 1: Attach the Selfie Stick

Select the Right Stick:

Use the official Insta360 Invisible Selfie Stick, which is designed to be thin and to minimize visibility in the camera's field of view.

Attach the Camera:

Screw the Insta360 X4 onto the top of the selfie stick securely. Ensure it's tightly fastened to prevent any wobbling or detachment.

Step 2: Positioning the Selfie Stick

Vertical Position:

Hold or extend the selfie stick vertically. The software is optimized to remove the stick when it is held straight and close to the camera body.

Keep It Steady:

While the selfie stick is invisible, movements can still affect video stability. Keep your hand steady to maintain smooth footage.

Using the Invisible Selfie Stick Feature

Step 1: Enable the Feature

Camera Settings:

The Insta360 X4 automatically detects and removes the selfie stick from the footage. There's no need to manually enable this feature as it is built into the camera's stitching algorithm.

Step 2: Capture Footage

Recording Videos:

Use the selfie stick to capture videos from unique angles. Walk around with the stick extended or rotate it to capture dynamic, immersive footage.

Ensure you maintain a vertical orientation to keep the selfie stick invisible.

Taking Photos:

Use the selfie stick to capture 360-degree photos. Hold the stick vertically and position it to capture the desired scene.

Step 3: Review and Edit

Review Footage:

Review your footage on the Insta360 app or Insta360 Studio. The invisible selfie stick feature should automatically remove the stick from your shots.

Editing:

Use the Insta360 app or Insta360 Studio to further enhance your footage. Apply stabilization, adjust the framing, and add effects as needed.

WHEN TO USE THE INVISIBLE SELFIE STICK

Action Shots:

Sports and Activities:

Use the invisible selfie stick during activities like skiing, snowboarding, biking, or hiking to capture immersive action shots without the distraction of the stick in the frame.

Dynamic Movement:

The stick allows you to get close to the action while keeping the focus on the subject and surroundings.

Travel and Adventures:

Landscapes and Scenery:

Capture stunning landscapes and scenic views while traveling. The invisible selfie stick provides a wide field of view without any obstructions.

Vlogging

Create engaging vlogs by holding the selfie stick out in front of you. This creates a floating camera effect, making your videos look professional and immersive.

Creative Angles:

Unique Perspectives:

Experiment with different angles and perspectives. Extend the selfie stick to capture aerial-like views or place it in unique positions to get creative shots.

Group Photos:

Take group photos without the need for a tripod. The selfie stick can capture everyone in the shot without appearing in the photo.

Events and Gatherings:

Parties and Celebrations:

Document events and gatherings with ease. The invisible selfie stick allows you to move around and capture candid moments without the stick appearing in the footage.

Weddings and Special Occasions:

Use the stick to capture 360-degree views of weddings and special occasions, providing a comprehensive record of the event.

By using the invisible selfie stick feature, you can enhance your 360-degree content, making it more immersive and visually appealing. Experiment with different scenarios and techniques to get the most out of this innovative feature on your Insta360 X4.

COMPETITION AND LAST THOUGHTS

There's competition, mostly from Ricoh's Theta 360 cameras and GoPro's GoPro Max 360 camera. But Insta360's feature set and easy-to-use editing interface shine. At the moment, Insta360 is the sole manufacturer of 360-degree cameras aimed at consumers that provide actual 8K resolution.

A robust and efficient imaging platform is the Insta360 X4. As everything around the camera is recorded, it enables the photographer to document an event without thinking about where to point it. You may edit stunning "regular" videos, take stills, or produce immersive 360-degree YouTube videos.

The Insta360 X4 has an astounding amount of creative possibilities with features like "me mode" tracking, a level horizon option, and a bigger battery for longer recording times. I suggest utilizing a 1TB or at least 512GB V30 U3 A2 micro-SD card for the longest possible recording period.

All things considered, the Insta360 X4 is an amazing technological device that provides an entertaining and creative approach to record and sharing your journeys and other experiences.

The Insta360 X4 guarantees you to record the joy and feeling of your activities in a way never possible whether you're driving, diving, flying, or traveling.

THE END

www.ingramcontent.com/pod-product-compliance
Lightning Source LLC
Chambersburg PA
CBHW050209230526
45470CB00001B/304

Samsung Galaxy A15 Manual For Beginners And Seniors

A Complete Manual With Tips & Tricks On How To Use And Master Your Samsung Galaxy A15 Mobile Phone.

Michael Donald